ACTIONS SPEAK
LOUDER THAN BUMPER STICKERS

Edited by Olivia Greer & Aaron Rudenstine

NATION BOOKS
NEW YORK

ACTIONS SPEAK LOUDER THAN BUMPER STICKERS

Published by
Nation Books
An Imprint of Avalon Publishing Group, Inc.
245 West 17th Street, 11th Floor
New York, NY 10011

AVALON
publishing group incorporated

Nation Books is a co-publishing venture of the Nation Institute and Avalon Publishing Group, Incorporated.

Library of Congress Cataloging-in-Publication Data is available.

ISBN-10: 1-56025-942-6
ISBN-13: 978-1-56025-942-8

9 8 7 6 5 4 3 2 1

Book design by Michael Fusco
Printed in China
Distributed by Publishers Group West

ACKNOWLEDGMENTS

This book would not be in your hands without the help of many people.

We'd like to pay tribute to the imagination of the bumper sticker creators whose work is featured here, and thank them for their belief in this project: Bumper Art, Bumper Talk, Carry A Big Sticker, Flying Spaghetti Monster, I Evolved, Irregular Times, Northern Sun, Share the Satire, and The Bumper Sticker.

Our great thanks to David Korzenik and Stephen Bailey for giving so generously of their time and legal expertise.

We are indebted to Michael Fusco for an exceptional cover design and for going above and beyond the call of duty in laying out the book. Whitney Hess dragged us out of the Stone Age and provided invaluable tech support. Thanks also to Ellen Lerner, our printing guru, for guiding us through the process.

We are so lucky to have had extraordinary advice along the way: Claudia Chaback, Ellen Chesler, Rupali Chopra, Elizabeth Cooke, Susan Davis, Janet Goldstein, Marci Hamilton, Don Hazen, Mark Kornblau, Reynold Levy, Matt Mallow, Mark Nichols, Behram Panthaki, Beata Pudelko, Fern Reiss, Sarah Robinson, and Johnny Temple.

In developing factoids and choosing bumper stickers, we are grateful to our friends: Elliott Appel, Megan Dullaghan, Justin Erlich, Rosha Forman, Adam Frankel, Caleb Hurst-Hiller, Jennifer Keiser, Betsy Mallow, Sara Mckinley, Jeremy Robbins, Gui Stampur, and Lauren Wiener.

Special thanks go to our families – Colin, David, Franny, Lucy, Sasha, Sharna, Simon, and Zina – who have worn many hats: thoughtful sounding boards, founts of advice, careful editors, and loving supporters.

INTRODUCTION

These bumper stickers make us laugh...and then they make us wince. Each one pokes fun at deeper truths with real implications for our lives and our society.

From Bush bashing to economics, abortion to the military, creationism to the environment, these bumper stickers speak to today's hot button issues, making fun of just about everything. And when the laughter peaks, it's compounded by a tidbit of truth appearing next to it – a "factoid" that grounds the joke in reality.

Humor offers a removed observation on sometimes-painful truths, and lets us stroll around reality a bit before we move in for a closer look. In high school, when our friends were making fun of each other, they used to say, "it's funny cuz it's true." Similarly, these bumper stickers take their humor from the truths they mock, and as we began to compile them, we saw that they might inspire not just laughter, but also reflection and engagement.

We envision this book sitting on any coffee table, kitchen table, or dorm room desk, and acting as a catalyst for participation. This is hilarious political commentary that encourages laughter and thought, the combination of which we believe invites action – from conversation to provocation.

When we began, in a pretty somber – perhaps even dire – political climate, we wanted to laugh, and we wanted to make other people laugh. As we proceeded, our desire for laughter developed into a desire for action. Actions do speak louder than bumper stickers, and as the humor keeps us human, the action keeps our society humane.

We're New York City progressives, born and raised. We're in our twenties. We have jobs and dreams that don't always intersect as we'd like them to. Clearly, we have a specific worldview. We struggle to digest the realities of today's political climate, and we work to figure out how to live with it and how to make a difference. We talk with our friends, our families, our co-workers and our mentors. At times we feel hopeless and at times we feel tremendously empowered.

We harbor no illusions that this book will change the course of America. But we do intend it to keep us wincing, and we intend it to spark conversations, debates, and even arguments. Above all, we hope it will inspire readers to laugh their way into action.

Olivia Greer & Aaron Rudenstine
New York City, October 2005
An original publication of **ACTIONS SPEAK LOUDER**

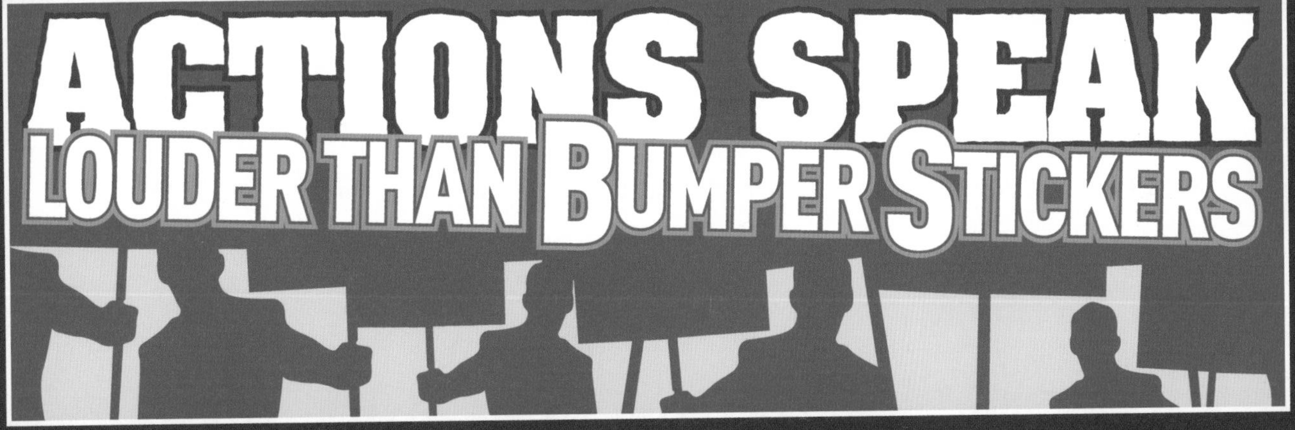
ACTIONS SPEAK
LOUDER THAN BUMPER STICKERS

2000 Election Results

Candidate	Vote (#)	Vote (%)
Bush	50,456,169	48
Gore	50,996,116	48

2004 Election Results

Candidate	Vote (#)	Vote (%)
Bush	62,040,606	51
Kerry	59,028,109	48

Dear World,
Sorry. We tried our best.
— Half of America

http://www.cafepress.com/ievolved
ellieartstuff@yahoo.com

On June 16, 2004, the 9/11 Commission reported that it found "no collaborative relationship" between Iraq and al Qaeda.

Even so, as of September 2004, 42% of Americans still believed that Saddam Hussein's regime in Iraq was *directly* involved in planning, financing, or carrying out the terrorist attacks of 9/11.

if ignorance were truly bliss
Americans would be ecstatic

©BumperTalk.com

BD104A

http://www.bumpertalk.com/bumpertalk/BD104A.html

Number of female Members of Congress: **83**

Number of male Members of Congress: **452**

Number of women who have abortions in the United States each year: **1.31 million**

Number of men who have abortions in the United States each year: **0**

If you cut off my reproductive choice, can I cut off yours?

From 2001 to 2003, at the 50 American firms outsourcing the most service jobs, CEOs earned $2.2 billion, while sending an estimated 200,000 jobs overseas.

In 2003, at the 50 American firms outsourcing the most service jobs, average CEO compensation increased by 46%, compared to a 9% average increase for all CEOs.

Our factories are all overseas
All we produce here are
RICH EXECUTIVES

The political terms **Left and Right** referred originally to the seating arrangements of the various legislative bodies during the French Revolutionary era. The aristocracy and other supporters of the monarchy sat to the right of the Speaker; commoners and other supporters of reform sat to the left.

SLOWER MINDS KEEP RIGHT

© 2005 Northern Sun Merchandising   Minneapolis MN 55406   www.northernsun.com   800-258-8579   7042

For 2006, Congress authorized $22.75 billion for Title I of the No Child Left Behind Act. President George W. Bush requested only $13.3 billion of that total, continuing a pattern of underfunding education. Adding $9 billion to reach the authorized level of funding would have provided the resources needed to improve more than 1,700 secondary schools that struggle to meet standards.

For 2006, President Bush requested $419.3 billion for the Department of Defense.

It will be a great day when our SCHOOLS get all the MONEY they need and the AIR FORCE has to hold a BAKE SALE to buy a BOMBER.

Evidence suggests that during the 2000 Presidential election, electronic voting machines in Florida awarded George W. Bush up to 260,000 more votes than he should have received. In Palm Beach County, due to defects in the ballot form, at least 2,000 people who intended to vote for Al Gore actually voted for Pat Buchanan, while virtually no votes intended for Bush went to another candidate.

Bush won Florida by 537 votes.

One Person, One Vote
(offer not valid in Florida)

BD041A

48% of Americans believe that humans and other living things have evolved over time.

42% of Americans believe that humans and other living things have existed in their present form since the beginning of time.

10% of Americans don't know.

http://www.cafepress.com/ievolved
ellieartstuff@yahoo.com

The federal minimum wage is **$5.15** per hour.

The federal government defines poverty as **$19,223** annually for a family of four.

In order to reach the poverty line in America, a minimum wage worker needs to work **72** hours per week, **52** weeks per year.

In 2004, **37** million Americans lived below the poverty line.

¢apitali$m:
The predatory phase
of human development

In January 2005, polling in 44 countries revealed that the world is "deeply suspicious of U.S. motives and openly skeptical about its word." Anti-Americanism is "deeper and broader now than at any time in modern history," even in countries that have been close U.S. allies for over 50 years.

We are creating enemies faster than we can kill them

© 2003 Northern Sun Merchandising   Minneapolis MN 55406   www.northernsun.com   800-258-8579   5632

The Census found 594,000 same sex partner households in 2000, all of whom pay taxes at the same rate as all other Americans and are subject to the same laws.

Yet, because same sex couples are unable to marry, they are denied the basic rights and protections that heterosexual couples benefit from:

- Spousal health insurance benefits.
- The right to make medical decisions on behalf of a spouse.
- Residency for a foreign spouse of a U.S. citizen.
- Joint child custody.
- Award of child custody in divorce proceedings.
- The right to inherit from a spouse who dies.
- Social Security survivor's benefits.

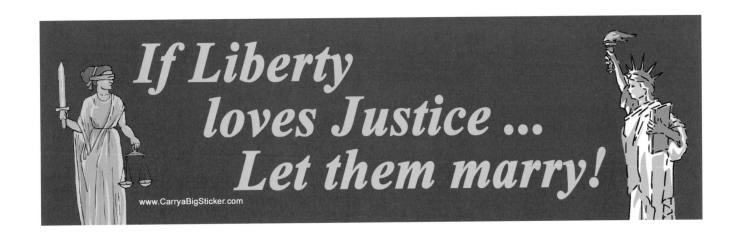

If Liberty loves Justice ... Let them marry!

www.CarryaBigSticker.com

"Capital punishment is our society's recognition of the sanctity of human life."

(Senator Orrin Hatch, R - UT)

"I have enormous personal ambition. I want to shift the entire planet. And I'm doing it. I am now a famous person." *(House Speaker Newt Gingrich, R - GA)*

"Let me tell you something about this AIDS epidemic. There is not one single case of AIDS reported in this country that cannot be traced in origin to sodomy."

(Senator Jesse Helms, R - NC)

"Women are hard enough to handle now without giving them a gun."
(Senator Barry Goldwater, R - AZ, talking about women in the armed services)

———

"Suppose you were an idiot. And suppose you were a member of Congress. But, I repeat myself."

-- Mark Twain

© LibertyStickers.com 877-873-9626

www.libertystickers.com

29

Since 2000, the number of registered lobbyists in Washington has more than doubled to nearly 35,000.

In 2004, lobbyists received $2.14 billion from corporations, industries, and other special interest groups.

Between 2000 and 2005, 628 members of Congress took 6,242 trips at the expense of private organizations.

INVEST IN AMERICA

BUY A CONGRE$$MAN

©BumperTalk.com

BD024A

http://www.bumpertalk.com/bumpertalk/BD024A.html

"There are things we know we know, and that's helpful to know you know something. There are things we know we don't know. And that's really important to know, and not think you know them, when you don't. But the tricky ones are the ones - the unknown unknowns - the things we don't know we don't know. They're the ones that can get you in a bucket of trouble."

(Donald Rumsfeld, Secretary of Defense, December 2003)

The Nixon Tapes capture a number of talks between President Richard Nixon and Donald Rumsfeld, then Director of the Office of Economic Opportunity. In one conversation, Nixon muses that the only cabinet position Rumsfeld would not be fit for is Secretary of Defense.

There are known knowns.
There are known unknowns.
There are unknown knowns.
There are unknown unknowns.
As we know.

ShareTheSatire.com

- Rumsfeldian Mantra

The Union of Concerned Scientists, made up of more than 60 leading scientists – Nobel laureates, leading medical experts, former federal agency directors, and university chairs and presidents – has written an open letter denouncing the Bush Administration's suppression of scientific inquiry.

The letter claims:

- The Administration has manipulated its scientific advisory system to suppress advice that might run counter to their political agenda.
- The Administration has censored government scientists on "sensitive" topics.
- The Administration's abuse of science has reached a level of unprecedented proportions.

Artificial Intelligence is no match for Natural Stupidity.

During President Bill Clinton's first **52** months in office, **11,971,000** private sector jobs were created, at a growth rate of **13.2%**.

During President Bush's first **52** months in office, **24,000** jobs were lost, at a growth rate of **-0.02%**.

President Bush is the first president since Herbert Hoover to finish an entire term in office with a net loss of private sector jobs.

The Equal Rights Amendment has been introduced in every session of Congress since 1923, but has not been ratified. It reads:

Section 1. Equality of Rights under the law shall not be denied or abridged by the United States or any state on account of sex.

Section 2. The Congress shall have the power to enforce, by appropriate legislation, the provisions of this article.

Section 3. This amendment shall take effect two years after the date of ratification.

Feminism is the radical notion that women are people

In 1981, the UN Security Council passed a resolution arguing that if preemptive strike were accepted as legal, any state could attack another under the pretext that it detected a threat.

The United States supported the resolution.

In June 2002, President Bush introduced the doctrine of "preemptive action," and justified the war in Iraq on the "pretext" that Iraq was developing weapons of mass destruction. That pretext has been proven false.

Love your neighbor pre-emptively

www.CarryaBigSticker.com (928) 774-5942

In 2001, the Bush Administration pulled out of the Kyoto Treaty, citing potential harm to the U.S. economy.

The Administration proposed an alternate plan for reducing U.S. emissions **18%** by **2012,** but the General Accounting Office has found that the program will actually result in just a **2%** drop by **2012.**

Have you heard the one about Global Warming?

ShareTheSatire.com

President Bush has remarked: "The reason we are where we are, in terms of the deficit, is because we went through a recession, we were attacked, and we're fighting a war."

Yet, studies show that Bush's tax cuts are the largest single factor contributing to the deficit, accounting for **35%** of the expected **$9.3 trillion** budget deficit over the next **10 years.**

The cost of Bush's tax cuts:

- 30 times the Environment Protection Agency's budget.
- 5 times the cost of programs operated by the Department of Housing and Urban Development.
- 4 times the amount spent on education.
- 4 times the amount spent on veterans.

Democrats think the glass is half full.
Republicans think the glass is **theirs.**

In 1933, Franklin Delano Roosevelt stood before a nation in the throes of the Great Depression and said: "the only thing we have to fear is fear itself."

In 2002, American leaders stood before a nation confronting terrorism and said:

Another terrorist attack is "not a matter of if, but when."

(Vice President Dick Cheney)

Suicide bombings in public places in America are "inevitable."

(FBI Director Robert Mueller)

"We do face additional terrorist threats. And the issue is not if but when and where and how." *(Secretary of Defense Donald Rumsfeld)*

FDR: We have nothing to fear but fear itself.

BUSH: Orange Alert! Duct Tape! *Irregular Times*

Before George W. Bush was elected president:

- He went AWOL from the National Guard during a time of war.

- As owner of the Texas Rangers, he traded Sammy Sosa to the Chicago Cubs.

- He sat on the board of Harken Energy while it set up an offshore tax dodge.

- He triggered an SEC investigation into possible insider trading when he unloaded $835,000 worth of Harken Energy shares about two months before Harken announced a big loss.

- His candidacy for commissioner of Major League Baseball was rejected.

SOMEWHERE IN TEXAS THERE'S A VILLAGE MISSING AN IDIOT

The Bush Administration:

- Hid the identity of oil executives who helped create America's energy policy.

- Condoned abuse by U.S. armed forces.

- Appointed unqualified people to lead major federal agencies.

- Awarded no-bid contracts to politically connected corporations.

- Suppressed scientific evidence that ran counter to its political goals.

President Bush's Executive Order 13233 mandates that a former president's private papers can only be released with the approval of that president (or his heirs) and the current president.

This order ensures that the actions of the Bush Administration (and others) will go unexamined.

The truth is out there
it sure isn't anywhere around here

©BumperTalk.com

BC401A

http://www.bumpertalk.com/bumpertalk/BC401A.html

On July 6, 2003, former U.S. Ambassador Joseph C. Wilson publicly disputed the White House's claim that Saddam Hussein had sought to buy uranium from Niger for possible use in a nuclear weapon.

On July 8 or 9, 2003, President Bush's top political advisor, Karl Rove, had a conversation with conservative columnist Robert D. Novak, in which Rove is believed to have confirmed the identity of Wilson's wife, Valerie Plame.

On July 14, 2003, Novak published an article exposing Plame as an undercover CIA operative.

Leaking the identity of an undercover CIA operative is a **"betrayal of national security"** and, under certain circumstances, a **felony.**

In 2004, America's **257,000** millionaires received an average of **$136,398** each in tax cuts.

The poorest **20%** of Americans received an average of **$19** each.

Congress gave huge tax breaks to the rich and all I got was this lousy bumpersticker

In March 2003, President Bush launched Operation Iraqi Freedom, with the professed goal of "a free and prosperous Iraq."

Since the start of the war:

- An estimated 40,000 Iraqi civilians have been killed.

- On average, 155 Iraqi security forces have died each month.

- More than 2,000 American soldiers have been killed.

- In 2005, operations costs in Iraq are estimated at $5.6 billion per month.

Two years after the initial invasion of Iraq, the country endures ongoing violence. In the first five months of 2005, suicide attack rates rose to 50 per month, compared to 20 per month in 2003.

Be nice to America
Or we'll bring democracy
to your country.

www.CarryaBigSticker.com

In 1990, Kentucky extended a 1976 law allowing public schools to teach creationism in the classroom.

In 1996, Alabama added a disclaimer to biology textbooks, describing evolution as a "controversial theory."

In 1999, the Kansas Board of Education removed most references to evolution from its curriculum.

In 2002, biology textbooks in Cobb County, Georgia, were labeled with a disclaimer stating that evolution is "a theory, not a fact."

In 2005, school officials in Beebe, Arkansas, placed a sticker in high school textbooks questioning the theory of evolution.

In 2005, the Dover School Board in Pennsylvania mandated that the school library carry "Of Pandas and People," a book that introduces intelligent design as a valid alternative to evolution.

President Bush signed the **USA Patriot Act** into law on October 26, 2001. Under the Patriot Act:

- The government can force any person or institution - including doctors, libraries, bookstores, universities, and Internet service providers - to turn over their clients' or customers' records.

- The government can conduct searches with no immediate obligation to notify the subject.

- The government can secretly conduct physical searches or wiretaps on American citizens without proving probable cause.

- Non-citizens can be held indefinitely without trial.

President of the United States, George W. Bush:

"Too many good docs are getting out of business. Too many OB/GYNs aren't able to practice their love with women all across this country."

(September 2004, Poplar Bluff, MS)

"We look forward to analyzing and working with legislation that will make – it would hope – put a free press's mind at ease that you're not being denied information you shouldn't see."

(April 2005, Washington DC)

"Our enemies are innovative and resourceful, and so are we. They never stop thinking about new ways to harm our country and our people, and neither do we."

(August 2004, Washington DC)

"See, in my line of work you got to keep repeating things over and over and over again for the truth to sink in, to kind of catapult the propaganda."

(May 2005, Greece, NY)

My Kid is an Honor Student
My President is a Moron

Between 2000 and 2004, the number of uninsured Americans grew by 6 million.

In 2004, 45.8 million Americans lived without health insurance.

Since 2000, health insurance premiums for insured Americans have risen by an average rate of 12.5% each year.

Between 2000 and 2005, due to rising costs, the number of working Americans with job-based insurance dropped from 63.6% to 59.8%.

OUR NATIONAL / DON'T HEALTH PLAN / GET SICK

© 2002 Northern Sun Merchandising   Minneapolis MN 55406   www.northernsun.com   800-258-8579   5890

At an April 2004 press conference, President Bush assured Americans: "had we had any inkling that this [9/11] was going to happen, we would have done everything in our power to stop the attack."

Yet in August 2001, Bush received a memo from the CIA, titled "Bin Laden Determined to Attack America." He remained in Crawford, TX, and continued his month-long vacation.

At the same **2004** press conference, Bush was asked to identify any "errors in judgment" he may have made in relation to 9/11.

He responded: "You know, I just – I'm sure something will pop into my head here in the midst of this press conference, with all the pressure of trying to come up with an answer, but it hadn't yet [sic]."

Being in government means never having to say you're sorry.

© *LibertyStickers.com* 877-873-9626

Each year in the United States:

- 9.1 million 15-24 year olds are infected with a sexually transmitted disease.

- More than 800,000 15-19 year old girls become pregnant.

Studies show that most abstinence-only-until-marriage programs fail to prevent teens from having sex before marriage, and actually deter teens from using condoms and getting tested for STDs once they start having sex.

Since President Bush took office, he has increased annual funding for abstinence-only-until-marriage programs from $97.5 million to $270 million.

Abstinence is the leading cause of immaculate conceptions

www.CarryaBigSticker.com

Two thirds of all species make their homes in forests.

60 million people depend on forests for their homes and livelihoods.

Over **30 million** acres of forest are lost each year.

Daddy, what were trees like?

BumperArt.com

At the start of the 20th century, **10%-15%** of war casualties were civilians.

During World War II, more than **50%** of war casualties were civilians.

By the end of the 20th century, over **75%** of war casualties were civilians.

Fighting for peace is like screwing for virginity

BumperArt.com

On May 1, 2003, President Bush landed a Navy S-3B Viking on the USS Abraham Lincoln. Under a sign reading "Mission Accomplished," Bush announced that major combat operations in Iraq had ended.

As of September 30, 2005, the Coalition death toll in Iraq was **2,131**, including **1,936** Americans. More than **85%** of these deaths occurred after President Bush's announcement that major combat was over.

"Yeehaw!" is not a foreign policy.

In July 2005, the United States Congress passed a highway bill in which a total of $24 billion was earmarked for a record-breaking 6,376 "special projects." $223 million was allotted to Alaska for a bridge that would connect the town of Ketchikan (pop. 8,900) to Gravina Island (pop. 50), replacing a 10-minute ferry ride that has worked for years. **The bridge will serve so few people, it would be more economical to buy each one a private plane.**

I don't like political jokes
too many get elected

©BumperTalk.com

BD493A

http://www.bumpertalk.com/bumpertalk/BD493A.html

ANSWER: 59,439,413*

* Represents the **59,028,109** who voted for John Kerry, plus the 411,304 who voted for Ralph Nader, in the 2004 election.

As of September 2005, Bush's approval ratings had dropped to their lowest point of his presidency – **57%** of all Americans disapproved of his performance. If Bush's train left Washington then, **69,243,611** Americans would have started to cheer.

WORD PROBLEM:
If George W. Bush leaves Washington on a train at a speed of 50 MPH, how many million Americans will start cheering?

During the 2004 Presidential campaign, Alan Keyes, former Republican candidate for the Senate, publicly denounced Vice President Dick Cheney's lesbian daughter, Mary Cheney, as a "selfish hedonist."

Months later, upon learning that his own daughter, Maya Keyes, was a lesbian, Keyes and his wife "threw her out of their house, refused to pay her college tuition, and stopped speaking to her."

I'm Gay. You're an Asshole.

I Was Born This Way. You'll Die That Way.

BumperArt.com

In 1828, when Andrew Jackson ran for president, his critics called him a "jackass" for his populist views and his slogan, "Let the people rule." Jackson used the name calling to his advantage, featuring the donkey on his campaign posters. During his presidency, the donkey was used to represent Jackson's stubbornness. The symbol came to represent the Democratic Party.

In 1874, the New York Herald derided President Ulysses S. Grant's possible third-term run with a cartoon of a donkey in a lion's skin frightening away all the animals in the forest, and a headline of "Caeserism." The caption read: "An ass having put on a lion's skin roamed about in the forest and amused himself by frightening all the foolish animals he met within his wanderings." One of the "foolish animals" was an elephant, representing the Republican vote. The symbol came to represent the Republican Party.

BIPARTISANSHIP
I'll hug your elephant if you kiss my ass

© 2002 Northern Sun Merchandising   Minneapolis MN 55406   www.northernsun.com   800-258-8579   5524

President Andrew Johnson dismissed Secretary of War Edwin Stanton without the approval of the Senate, as required in the Tenure of Office Act. He was impeached.

President Richard Nixon conspired to cover up a major political scandal in his White House. The House of Representatives initiated impeachment proceedings, but Nixon resigned his office before he was impeached.

President Bill Clinton denied his adulterous affair with a White House intern, while under oath. He was impeached.

President George W. Bush:

- Justified war in Iraq based on the threat of weapons of mass destruction. Weapons were never found.

- Justified war in Iraq based on Saddam Hussein's ties to al Qaeda. No evidence of these ties has been found.

President Bush has not been impeached.

Give Impeachment a Chance

ShareTheSatire.com

In 2005, a "Stench of Corruption" emanates from Capitol Hill:

House Majority Leader Tom Delay is indicted on a felony charge that he conspired to launder corporate campaign contributions.

Senate Majority Leader Bill Frist comes under investigation by both the Justice Department and the Securities and Exchange Commission for insider trading.

Republican lobbyist Jack Abramoff, known for his close ties to Karl Rove and Tom Delay, is indicted with a business partner on wire and conspiracy fraud.

Vice President Dick Cheney's chief of staff, I. Lewis "Scooter" Libby, is charged with five criminal counts relating to the leaked identity of CIA operative Valerie Plame.

Politicians and Diapers Need to be changed
Often for the same reasons

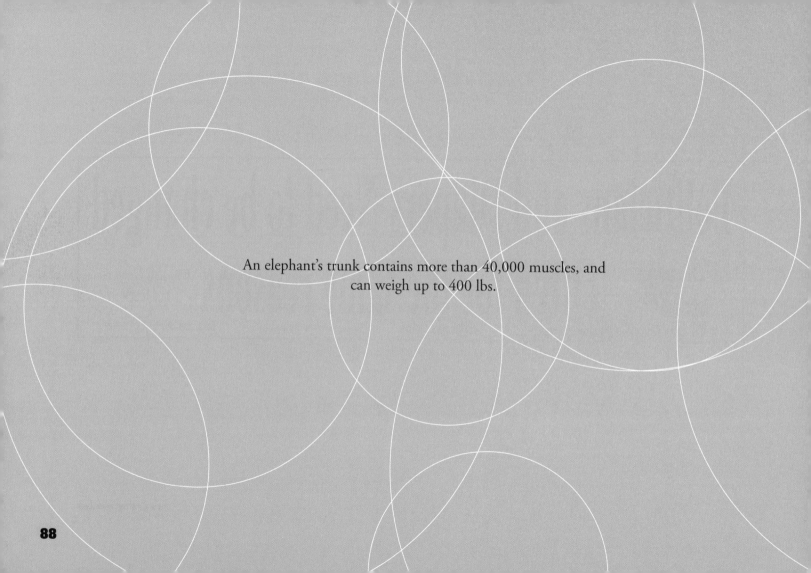

An elephant's trunk contains more than 40,000 muscles, and can weigh up to 400 lbs.

ENDNOTES

Page 6: "President Results Summary for All States," *CNN*. Cited 8 October 2005. URL: http://www.cnn.com/ELECTION/2000/results/index.president.html; "Election Results," *CNN*. Cited 8 October 2005. URL: www.cnn.com/ELECTION/2004/pages/results/president/.

Page 8: Pincus, Walter and Dana Milbank, "Al Qaeda Hussein Link Is Dismissed," *The Washington Post*, 17 June 2004; "Newsweek Poll conducted by Princeton Survey Research Associates," *The Polling Report*, 2-3 September 2004. Cited 8 October 2005. URL: http://www.pollingreport.com/iraq4.htm.

Page 10: "Questions and Answers About Congress," *U.S. Congressman Chaka Fattah*. Cited 8 October 2005. URL: http://www.house.gov/fattah/features/faq.htm; "Women In The United States Congress: 1917-2005," *Congressional Research Service*, 21 June 2005. Cited 8 October 2005. URL: http://www.senate.gov/reference/resources/pdf/RL30261.pdf; "Choosing Abortion — Questions and Answers," *Planned Parenthood*. Cited 9 October 2005. URL: http://www.plannedparenthood.org/pp2/portal/files/portal/medicalinfo/abortion/pub-abortion-q-and-a.xml.

Page 12: "Executive Excess," *United for a Fair Economy*, 31 August 2004. Cited 8 October 2005. URL: http://www.faireconomy.org/press/2004/EE2004_pr.html.

Page 14: "Left-Wing Politics," *Wikipedia*. Cited 8 October 2005. URL: http://en.wikipedia.org/wiki/Left-wing_politics#History_of_the_term.

Page 16: "Funding," *American Federation of Teachers*. Cited 8 October 2005. URL: http://www.aft.org/topics/nclb/funding.htm; "Fiscal Year 2006 Budget Summary," *White House Office of Management & Budget*. Cited 8 October 2005. URL: http://www.whitehouse.gov/omb/budget/fy2006/defense.html.

Page 18: Kim Zetter, "Researchers: Florida Vote Fishy," *Wired Magazine*, 18 November 2004. Cited 8 October 2005. URL: http://www.wired.com/news/evote/0,2645,65757,00.html; Henry E. Brady, "Report on Voting and Ballot Form in Palm Beach County," *University of California, Berkeley*. Cited 8 October 2005 URL: http://ucdata.berkeley.edu:7101/new_web/VOTE2000/palmbeachcoreport.pdf; "Florida," *CBS News*. Cited 8 October 2005. URL: http://www.cbsnews.com/campaign2000results/state/state_fl.html.

Page 20: "Public Divided on Origins of Life," *The Pew Forum on Religion and Public Life*, 30 August 2005. Cited 3 October 2005. URL: http://pewforum.org/docs/index.php?DocID=115#3.

Page 22: "Two Decades of Extraordinary Gains for Affluent Americans Yield Widest Income Gaps Since 1929," *Center on Budget and Policy Priorities*, 23 September 2003. Cited 8 October 2005. URL: http://www.cbpp.org/9-23-03tax-pr.htm; Bernstein, Jared and Isaac Shapiro, "Federal Minimum Wage Remains Unchanged for Eighth Straight Year, Falls to 56-Year Low Relative to the Average Wage," *Center on Budget and Policy Priorities*, Cited 8 October 2005. URL: http://www.cbpp.org/9-1-05mw.htm; Shipler, David K. *The Working Poor*. Knopf Publishing Group, 2005; "Federal Taxation of Earnings versus Investment Income in 2004," *Institute on Taxation & Economic Policy*, May 2004. Cited 8 October 2005. URL: http://www.itepnet.org/earnan.pdf.

Page 24: "Global Opinion: The Spread of Anti-Americanism," *Pew Research Center*, 24 January 2005. Cited 8 October 2005. URL: http://pewglobal.org/commentary/display.php?AnalysisID=104.

Page 26: "Married-Couple and Unmarried-Partner Households: 2000," *U.S. Census Bureau*, February 2003. Cited 10 October 2005. URL: http://www.census.gov/prod/2003pubs/censr-5.pdf; Board of Trustees, "Same Sex Marriage Resource Document (Retired)," *American Psychiatric Association*, December 1998. Cited 10 October 2005. URL: http://www.psych.org/edu/other_res/lib_archives/archives/199818.pdf; Board of Trustees, "Support of Legal Recognition of Same Sex Marriage Position Statement," *American Psychiatric Association*, May 2004. Cited 10 October 2005. URL: http://www.psych.org/edu/other_res/lib_archives/archives/200502.pdf; Bennet, Lisa and Gary Gates, "The Cost of Marriage Inequality to Gay, Lesbian and Bisexual Seniors," *The Urban Institute*, 21 January 2004. Cited 10 October 2005. URL: http://www.urban.org/url.cfm?ID=410939.

Page 28: Petras, Kathryn, and Ross Petras. *The Stupidest Things Ever Said By Politicians*. New York: Pocket Books, 1999.

Page 30: Frank Rich, "In the Beginning, there was Abramoff," *New York Times*, 2 October 2005; Jeffrey H. Birnbaum, "The Road to Riches is Called K Street," *The Washington Post*, 22 June 2005; Lou Dobbs, "Lobbying Against America" *CNN Money*, 11 August 2005. Cited 8 October 2005. URL: http://money.cnn.com/2005/08/11/commentary/dobbs/corporate_lobbying.

Page 32: "Excerpts: Rumsfeld interview," BBC, 14 June 2005. Cited 9 October 2005. URL: http://news.bbc.co.uk/2/hi/americans/4093762.stm; "The Life and Times of Donald Rumsfeld," *PBS Frontline*. Cited 8 October 2005. URL: http://www.pbs.org/wgbh/pages/frontline/shows/pentagon/etc/cronfeld.html.

Page 34: "Scientific Integrity in Policy Making," *Union of Concerned Scientists*, 18 February 2004. Cited 8 October 2005. URL: http://www.ucsusa.org/scientific_integrity/interference/reports-scientific-integrity-in-policy-making.html.

Page 36: Gene Sperling, "The Road to Zero: Still Not There Yet, Private Sector Job Growth Under President Bush," *Center for American Progress*, 3 June 2005. Cited 8 October 2005. URL: http://www.americanprogress.org/atf/cf/%7BE9245FE49A2B-43C7-A521-5D6FF2E06E03%7D/LONG_ROAD_TO_ZERO.PDF; "Bush Economic Record: The First Term," *Senate Joint Economic Committee*, 1 June 2005. Cited 8 October 2005. URL: http://jec.senate.gov/democrats/charts/ber_talkingpoints.pdf.

Page 38: "Equal Rights Amendment," *National Organization for Women*. Cited 8 October 2005. URL: http://www.now.org/issues/economic/eratext.html.

Page 40: "Foreign Policy In Focus Fact Sheet," *Foreign Policy in Focus*, 1 June 2002. Cited 8 October 2005. URL: http://www.fpif.org/students/firstmonday2002/factsheet2_body.html; "President Bush Delivers Graduation Speech at West Point," *The White House*, 1 June 2002. Cited 8 October 2005. URL: http://www.whitehouse.gov/news/releases/2002/06/20020601-3.html; Editorial, "Weapons That Weren't There," *The Washington Post*, 7 October 2004.

Page 42: "Text of a Letter from the President to Senators Hagel, Helms, Craig, and Roberts," *The White House*, 13 March 2001. Cited 8 October 2005. URL: http://www.whitehouse.gove/news/releases/2001/03/20010314.html; "Global Climate Change Policy Book," *The White House*, February 2002. Cited 8 October 2005. URL: http://www.whitehouse.gov/news/releases/2002/02/climatechange.html; "Preliminary Observations on the Administration's February 2002 Climate Initiative," General Accounting Office, 1 October 2003. Cited 8 October 2005. URL: http://http://www.gao.gov/new.items/d04131t.pdf; John Vidal, "Revealed: How Oil Giant Influenced Bush," *The Guardian*, 8 June 2005.

Page 44: "President Bush Discusses Budget After Cabinet Meeting," *The White House*, 2 February 2004. Cited 8 October 2005. URL: http://http://www.whitehouse.gov/news/releases/2004/02/20040202-1.html; Richard Kogan, "Deficit Picture Even Grimmer Than New CBO Projections Suggest," *Center on Budget and Policy Priorities*, 26 August 2003. Cited 8 October 2005. URL: http://www.cbpp.org/8-26-03bud.htm; Friedman, Joel, Ruth Carlitz, and David Kamin, "Extending the Tax Cuts Would Cost $2.1 Trillion Through 2015," *Center on Budget and Policy Priorities*, 9 February 2005. Cited15 October 2005. URL:http://www.cbpp.org/2-2-05tax.htm.

Page 46: "'Nothing to Fear but Fear Itself': FDR's First Inaugural Address," George Mason University. Cited 9 October 2005. URL: : http://historymatters.gmu.edu/d/5057; Risen, James and David Johnston, "U.S. Intercepting Messages Hinting At A New Attack," *The New York Times*, 19 May 2002; Kelly Wallace, "Lawmakers say new terrorist attack almost certain," *CNN*, 20 May 2002. Cited 8 October 2005. URL: http://archives.cnn.com/2002/ALLPOLITICS/05/20/terror.threats/; Zachary Coile, "FBI chief warns suicide attacks in U.S. 'inevitable.' Agency struggling to obtain intelligence on terror groups," *SF Gate*, 21 May 2002; "Transcript of testimony by Secretary of Defense Donald H. Rumsfeld at Defense Subcommittee of Senate Appropriations Committee," *United States Department of Defense*, 21 May 2002. Cited 8 October 2005. URL: http://www.defenselink.mil/speeches/2002/s20020521-secdef.html.

Page 48: Brooks Jackson, "Bush As Businessman," *CNN*, 13 May 1999. Cited 8 October 2005. URL: http://edition.cnn.com/ALLPOLITICS/stories/1999/05/13/president.2000/jackson.bush/; Howard Cole, "Sosa Trade A Steal," *Baseball Savvy*. Cited 8 October 2005. URL: http://http://www.baseballsavvy.com/archive/ob_SosaTradeASteal2.html; Lois Romano, "Bush's Guard Service In Question," *The Washington Post*, 3 February 2004; Tom Farrey, "Kicking Back and Getting Down To Business," *ESPN*, 2 November 2000. Cited 8 October, 2005. URL: espn.go.com/mlb/bush/wednesday.html; Robert L. Borosage, "Sacrifice is for Suckers," *The Nation*, 28 April 2003.

Page 50: Kitty Kelley, "Bush's Veil Over History," *The New York Times*, 10 October 2005.

Page 52: Mike Allen, "Rove Confirmed Plame Indirectly, Lawyer Says," *The Washington Post*, 15 July 2005; "Ex-Agents: CIA Leak A Serious Betrayal," *CNN*, 24 October 2003. Cited 8 October 2005. URL: http://www.cnn.com/2003/ALLPOLITICS/10/24/cnna.leak.

Page 54: Gale, William G., Peter R. Orszag, and Isaac Shapiro, "The Ultimate Burden of the Tax Cuts," *Center on Budget and Policy Priorities*, 2 June 2004. Cited 8 October 2005. URL: http://: http://www.cbpp.org/6-2-04tax.htm#_ftn1; Shapiro, Isaac, and Joel Friedman, "Tax Returns," *Center on Budget and Policy Priorities*, 23 April 2004. Cited 8 October 2004. URL: http://www.cbpp.org/4-14-04tax-sum.htm.

Page 56: "President Bush Addresses the Nation," *The White House*, 19 March 2003. Cited 10 October 2005. URL: http://www.whitehouse.gov/news/releases/2003/03/20030319-17.html; "President Discusses Operation Iraqi Freedom at Camp Lejeune," *The White House*, 3 April 2003. Cited 10 October 2005. URL: http://www.whitehouse.gov/news/releases/2003/04/20030403-3.html; Bennis, Phyllis and Erik Leaver and the IPS Iraq Task Force, "The Iraq Quagmire: The Mounting Costs of War and the Case for Bringing Home the Troops," *Institute for Policy Studies*, 31 August 2005. Cited 10 October 2005. URL: http://www.ips-dc.org/iraq/quagmire/; Kirk Semple, "Violence in Baghdad Includes Another Blast at Green Zone," *The New York Times*, 10 October 2005; "Casualties in Iraq," *Antiwar.com* Cited 29 October 2005. URL: http://www.antiwar.com/casualties.

Page 58: Tara Boyle, "Teaching Evolution: A State by State Debate," *NPR*, 4 May 2005. Cited 8 October 2005. URL: http://www.npr.org/templates/story/story.php?storyId=4630737; Michael Powell, "Pa. Case Is Newest Round in Evolution Debate," *The Washington Post*, 27 September 2005.

Page 60: American Civil Liberties Union, "Surveillance Under the U.S. Patriot Act," *American Civil Liberties Union*. Cited 8 October 2005. URL: http://www.aclu.org/SafeandFree/SafeandFree.cfm?ID=12263&c=206.

Page 62: "Remarks by the President on Teaching American History and Civic Education," *The White House*, 17 September 2002. Cited 8 October 2005. URL: http://www.whitehouse.gov/news/releases/2002/09/20020917-7.html; "President's Remarks at a Victory 2004 Rally in Poplar Bluff, Missouri," *The White House*, 6 September 2004. Cited 8 October 2005. URL: http://www.whitehouse.gov/news/releases/2004/09/20040906-4.html; "President Addresses American Society of Newspaper Editors Convention," *The White House*, 14 April 2005. Cited 8 October 2005. URL: http://www.

whitehouse.gov/news/releases/2005/04/20050414-4.html; "President Signs Defense Bill," *The White House*, 5 August 2004. Cited 8 October 2005. URL: http://www.whitehouse.gov/news/releases/2004/08/20040805-3.html; "President Participates in Social Security Conversation in New York," *The White House*, 24 May 2005. Cited 8 October 2005. URL: http://www.whitehouse.gov/news/releases/2005/05/20050524-3.html.

Page 64: "The Number of Uninsured Americans Continued to Rise in 2004," *Center for Budget and Policy Priorities*, 30 August 2005. Cited 8 October 2005. URL: http://www.cbpp.org/8-30-05health.htm; "Working But Uninsured: Millions of Employed Americans Uninsured and Unable to Get Medical Care," *Robert Wood Johnson Foundation*, 27 April 2005. Cited 8 October 2005. URL: http://www.rwjf.org/newsroom/newsreleasesdetail.jsp?id= 10347; Nicholas D. Kristof, "Medicine's Sticker Shock," *New York Times*, 2 October 2005.

Page 66: "President Addresses the Nation in Prime Time Press Conference," *The White House*, 13 April 2004. Cited 8 October 2005. URL: http://www.whitehouse.gov/news/releases/2004/04/20040413-20.html; Milbank, Dana and Mike Allen, "Bush Gave No Sign of Worry in August 2001," *The Washington Post*, 11 April 2004; "Transcript: Bin Laden determined to strike in US," *CNN*, 10 April 2004. Cited 8 October 2005. URL: http://www.cnn.com/2004/ALLPOLITICS/04/10/august6.memo/.

Page 68: "President Bush Risks Teen Lives by Increasing Funding For Dangerous Abstinence-Only Education," *Planned Parenthood*, 7 February 2005. Cited 8 October 2005. URL: http://www.plannedparenthood.org/pp2/portal/files/portal/media/pressreleases/pr-050207-abstinence.xml; "ACLU Announces Nationwide Action Aimed at Combating Dangerous Abstinence-Only-Until-Marriage Curricula in the States," *American Civil Liberties Union*, 21 September 2005. Cited 8 October 2005. URL: http://www.aclu.org/reproductiverights/reproductiverights.cfm?ID=19106&c=30.

Page 70: "Forests," *Natural Resources Defense Council*. Cited 8 October 2005. URL: http://www.nrdc.org/land/forests/default.asp; "Frequently Asked Questions," *Global Forest Watch*. Cited 8 October 2005. URL: http://www.globalforestwatch.org/english/about/faqs.htm.

Page 72: "The Ethics of War," *BBC*. Cited 8 October 2005. URL: http://www.bbc.co.uk/religion/ethics/war/justconduct2.shtml.

Page 74: "Commander In Chief Lands on USS Lincoln," *CNN*, 4 May 2003. Cited 8 October 2005. URL: http://www.cnn.com/2003/ALLPOLITICS/05/01/bush.carrier.landing/; "Forces: US & Coalition/Casualties," *CNN*. Cited 8 October 2005. URL: http://www.cnn.com/SPECIALS/2003/iraq/forces/casualties/; "Iraq Coalition Casualty Count," *Iraq Coalition Casualty Count*, Cited 8 October 2005. URL: http://icasualties.org/oif.

Page 76: Shailagh Murray, "After 2-Yr Wait, Passage Comes Early," *The Washington Post*, 30 July 2005; "Four Amendments & A Funeral," *Rolling Stone*, 25 August 2005.

Page 78: "Election Results 2004," *CNN*. Cited 8 October 2005. URL: http://www.cnn.com/ELECTION/2004/pages/results/president/; "President Bush's Approval Ratings 2005," *The Washington Post*, 8-11 September 2005. Cited 8 October 2005. URL: http://www.washingtonpost.com/wp-dyn/content/graphic/2005/04/25/GR2005042500945.html.

Page 80: "Keyes: Cheney's gay daughter practicing 'selfish hedonism'," *MSNBC*, 2 September 2004. Cited 8 October 2005. URL: http://www.msnbc.msn.com/id/5897569/; Marc Fisher, "When Sexuality Undercuts a Family's Ties," *The Washington Post*, February 13, 2005.

Page 82: "GOP History," *The Republican National Committee*. Cited 8 October 2005.
URL: http://www.gop.com/About/AboutRead.aspx?AboutType=3; "History of the Democratic Donkey," *The Democratic Party*. Cited 8 October 2005.
URL: http://www.democrats.org/a/2005/06/history_of_the.php.

Page 84: "Research Guide on Impeachment," *Library of Congress*. Cited 8 October 2005. URL: http://memory.loc.gov/ammem/amlaw/Impeachment-Guide.html; "Watergate: The Scandal That Brought Down Richard Nixon," *University of Illinois at Chicago: History of Impeachment*. Cited 8 October 2005. URL: http://www.uic.edu/depts/lib/documents/resources/history.shtml; Editorial, "Weapons That Weren't There," *The Washington Post*, 7 October 2004; "President Delivers State of the Union," *The White House*, 8 January 2003. Cited 8 October 2005. URL: http://www.whitehouse.gov/news/releases/2003/01/20030128-19.html; Dan Eggen, "No Evidence Connecting Iraq to Al Qaeda, 9/11 Panel Says," *The Washington Post*, 16 June 2004; Walter Pincus, "British Intelligence Warned of War," *The Washington Post*, 13 May 2005.

Page 86: Tim Grieve, "A Stench of Corruption," *Salon*, 28 September 2005. Cited 8 October 2005. URL: http://www.salon.com/politics/war_room/; Frank Rich, "In the Beginning, there was Abramoff," *The New York Times*, 2 October 2005; Squeo, Anne Marie and John D. McKinnon, "Top Cheney Aide Charged in Leak Inquiry," *The Wall Street Jounal*, 29 October 2005.

Page 88: "Quick Facts," *San Diego Zoo*. Cited 8 October 2005. URL: http://www.sandiegozoo.org/animalbytes/t-elephant.html; "Asian Elephant," *Oregon Zoo*. Cited 8 October 2005. URL: http://www.oregonzoo.org/Cards/Elephants/elephant.asian.htm.

To order additional copies of *Actions Speak Louder Than Bumper Stickers*, visit www.actionsspeaklouderthanbs.com.

Actions Speak Louder Than Bumper Stickers can be made available to non-profit organizations and institutions at reduced cost.

For information, please contact us at louderthanbs@gmail.com.